SINGAPORE

MAJOR WORLD NATIONS
SINGAPORE

Jessie Wee

CHELSEA HOUSE PUBLISHERS
Philadelphia

Chelsea House Publishers

3 5 7 9 8 6 4 2

brary of Congress Cataloging-in-Publication Data

Wee, Jessie.
Singapore / Jessie Wee.
p.   cm. — (Major world nations)
Includes index.
Summary: An introduction to the geography, history, economy, government,
people, and culture of the island republic that has been independent since
1965 and is located at the southern tip of the Malay Peninsula.
ISBN 0-7910-5397-0 (hc)
1. Singapore—Juvenile literature. [1. Singapore.] I. Wee, Jessie.
Let's visit Singapore. II Title. III. Series.
DS609.W44   1999
959.57—dc21   99-11870
CIP

ACKNOWLEDGEMENTS

The Author and Publishers are grateful to the following organizations and individuals
for permission to reproduce copyright photographs in this book:
Bedok North Primary School; Camerapix Hutchinson Ltd; Chris Fairclough;Corel
Galleria; The National Museum, Singapore; The Primary Production Department;The
Singapore Ministry of Defense; The Singapore Ministry of Health; The Singapore
Tourist Promotion Board; The Singapore Zoological Gardens and Travel Photo
International

CONTENTS

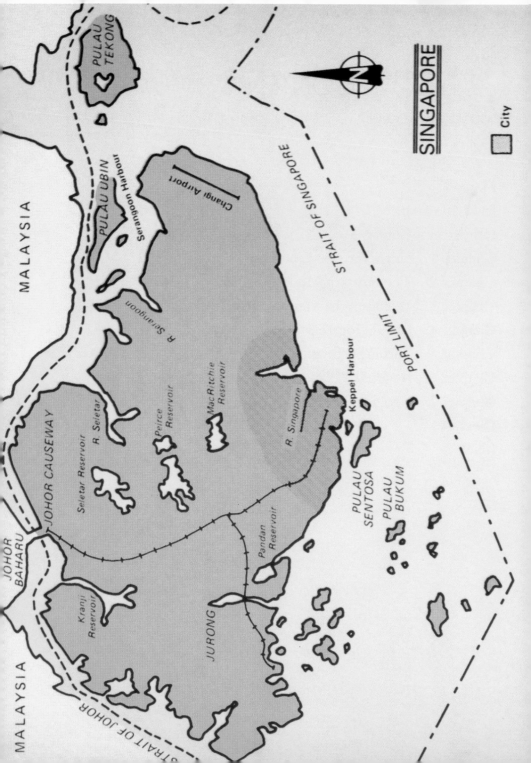

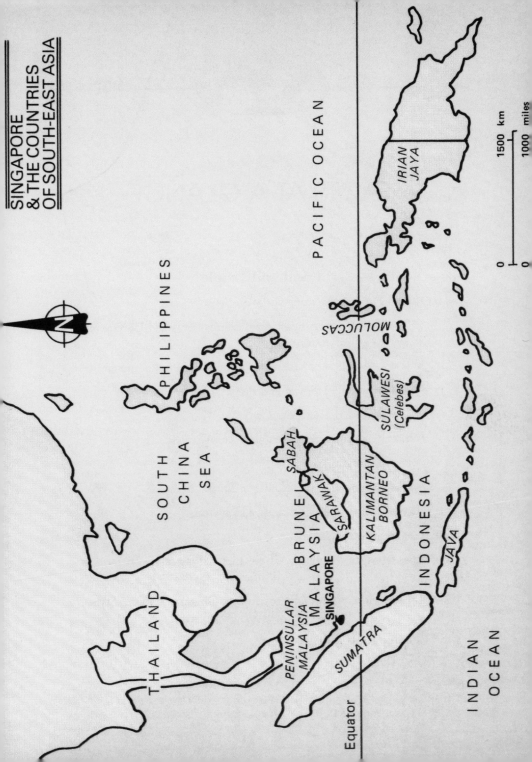

SINGAPORE
& THE COUNTRIES
OF SOUTH-EAST ASIA

PHILIPPINES

PACIFIC OCEAN

IRIAN JAYA

1500 km
1000 miles

MOLUCCAS

SOUTH
CHINA
SEA

SABAH

SULAWESI
(Celebes)

BRUNEI

SARAWAK

KALIMANTAN
BORNEO

THAILAND

MALAYSIA

INDONESIA

PENINSULAR
MALAYSIA

SINGAPORE

JAVA

SUMATRA

Equator

INDIAN
OCEAN

FACTS AT A GLANCE

Land and People

Official Name	Republic of Singapore
Location	Southeast Asia, islands between Malaysia and Indonesia
Area	414 square miles (647.5 square kilometers)
Climate	Tropical and rainy
Capital	Singapore City
Other Cities	Jurong, Bedok
Population	3,490,000
Major Rivers	Singapore River, Seletar River
Highest Point	Bukit Timah, 116 meters
Official Language	Malay
Other Languages	English, Chinese, Tamil (all of which are also considered official)
Religions	Buddhism, Muslim, Christian, Hindu, Sikh, Taoism, Confucianism
Literacy Rate	91.1 percent

Average Life Expectancy	78.49 years

Economy

Natural Resources	Fish, deep water ports
Division of Labor Force	Financial, business, 33.5 percent; manufacturing, 25.6 percent; commerce, 22.9 percent; construction, 6.6 percent
Agricultural Products	Rubber, copra, fruit, vegetables, poultry
Industries	Electronic, financial services, oil drilling equipment, petroleum refining, rubber processing
Major Imports	Aircraft, petroleum, chemicals
Major Exports	Computer equipment, rubber, petroleum products, telecommunication equipment
Major Trading Partners	Japan, Malaysia, United States, Thailand, South Korea
Currency	Singapore dollar

Government

Form of Government	Republic
Government Bodies	Parliament
Formal Head of State	President
Head of Government	Prime Minister

HISTORY AT A GLANCE

7th century A.D.   The Malays live in a settlement called Temasek at the mouth of the Singapore River.

14th century   Singa Pura is a thriving trading city with a walled fortress. War eventually breaks out over control of the Malay Peninsula and Singa Pura is destroyed.

1511   The Portuguese invade Malacca and its leader flees to Singa Pura to set up a new settlement.

1613   The Portuguese attack and destroy the Malaysian settlement.

1819   A British businessman, Sir Stamford Raffles, signs a treaty with a Malay chieftain, the Sultan of Jahore, to set up a trading post on the island at the mouth of the Singapore River.

1819-1824   Singapore grows from a small fishing village to a busy trading and distribution center.

1821   Chinese immigration to Singapore begins. The Chinese would eventually make-up the largest ethnic group on the island.

1822	Raffles appoints a committee to draw-up town plans for the city of Singapore.
1824	The British East India Company buys Singapore and all the islands around it.
1826	Penang, Malacca, and Singapore become known as the Straits Settlements and are all governed by the East India Company.
1867	Control of the Straits Settlements is taken over by the British government.
1869	The Suez Canal opening and the invention of steamships increases trade in Singapore. Singapore's population continues to increase at a high rate with many people from Malay, India, and China coming to the island to find employment.
1880	It is said of the varied population of Singapore that "48 races speak 54 languages." Large shipyards are built and Singapore becomes the world's largest exporter of rubber.
early 1900s	A railway line is built linking the north and south coasts of the island and eventually the mainland. Singapore becomes an important British military base.
1940s	With the likelihood of war with Japan increasing the British fortify the islands of Singapore and build up military bases.
1942	During World War II Japan captures Singapore with a surprise attack by land. Large numbers of civilians and military are sent to Changi Prison and prison camps in Malaya.

1945	British forces return after the Japanese surrender and a British Military Administration is set up to restore order.
1946	The Straits Settlements are dissolved. Penang and Malacca become part of Malaya, Singapore becomes a separate Crown Colony of Britain.
1948	The first elections are held to vote for six local members on the Legislative Council.
1957	The British government allows for an elected 51-member legislative assembly.
1959	Singapore is allowed internal self-government. Lee Kuan Yew becomes its first prime minister. The People's Action Party (PAP) wins an over-whelming majority in the legislative assembly which they would keep for at least the next forty years.
1961	The Federation of Malaysia is formed. It includes Singapore, Sabah, Sarawak, and the 11 states of Malaya. Singapore is an independent state within the Federation.
1960s-1980s	Under Lee Kuan Yew's tough and authoritative rule, Singapore rises from poverty to affluence with a thriving economy. The infrastructure is modernized and foreign investment encouraged.
1965	Singapore separates from the Malaysia federation and becomes an independent country.
1971	The last of the British military forces leave the island.
1981	For the first time a non-PAP member is elected to parliament.

1990   Lee Kuan Yew steps down as prime minister but remains influential behind the scenes becoming senior minister in the cabinet. Goh Chok Tong succeeds him.

1991   Opposition parties gradually gain a few seats in the parliament.

1993   Ong Teng Cheong becomes Singapore's first popularly elected president.

1994   Controversy over Singapore's harsh laws occurs when an American teenager is convicted of vandalism and sentenced to four months in jail and six strokes with a rattan cane.

1997   The Peoples's Action Party (PAP) again wins all but two seats in parliament. Questions are raised as to their tactics which are thought to be intimidating to the voting populace.

1

Singapore, the Lion City

Singapore is a young nation of 3.49 million people of different races, languages, religions, cultures, customs, and traditions. An independent republic since 1965, the island nation has, in a short span of time, transformed itself into a thriving and modern city state.

Today, Singapore is an important oil refining, blending, and distribution center. It has modern shipbuilding and repairing facilities and industries that supply the world with goods ranging from textiles to electronic products. It serves as a vital communications, financial, and banking center for Asia, and its port is the second busiest in the world.

Singapore's position at the crossroads of international sea and air routes, its free port status, cleanliness, well-stocked department stores, and hotels have attracted people from all over the world. Dubbed the "Garden Isle" because of its parks, trees, and flowers, Singapore has become Asia's most popular tourist stopover.

Part of the Japanese Garden—one of the many parks that have led to Singapore being called the Garden Isle.

Although much has been said and written about Singapore and its economic success, many people are still not quite sure of its exact location. They often say, "Singapore is in the Far East," and happily place tiny Singapore in Hong Kong, China, Japan, or even India!

Look at the land mass of Asia on a map of the world. In its southeastern corner is a long, thin finger of land running south to the equator. This stretch of land is the Malay Peninsula, known today as Peninsular Malaysia. It separates the Indian Ocean from

This park is known as the Chinese Garden—Chinese cultural influence is very strong in Singapore.

the South China Sea. Together with the line of islands to the south, it forms a sort of land bridge to Australia.

At the southern tip of the Malay Peninsula, across a narrow strip of water known as the Strait of Johor, is the island of Singapore. Since 1923, a bridge carrying a road, a railway, and a water pipeline has joined Singapore to the mainland. This bridge, the Johor Causeway, is about three-quarters of a mile (one kilometer) long.

The island of Singapore is situated at latitude one degree north and longitude 103 degrees, about 85 miles (137 kilometers) north of the equator. It lies at the entrance to the Strait of Malacca, the world's longest strait and Asia's busiest sea lane for ships traveling between the East and West.

Besides Thailand and Peninsular Malaysia in the north, and Brunei and the Malaysian states of Sabah and Sarawak in the east, Singapore's other neighbors include the scattered islands of Indonesia in the south and the islands of the Philippines in the northeast.

The Republic of Singapore is made up of a main island and about 60 offshore islands. A number of the offshore islands are little more than sandbanks. Some of the larger ones, such as Pulau Bukum, Pulau Sentosa, Pulau Tekong, and Pulau Ubin, are inhabited. These, and some other islands, are used as oil refineries, as recreational centers for Singaporeans and tourists, and as bases for military training. *Pulau* is the Malay word for island.

The main island of Singapore, shaped like a diamond or, as has been said, "like a bat with its wings outstretched," is 26 miles (42 kilometers) long and 14 miles (23 kilometers) wide. Together with the offshore islands within its territorial waters, the Republic of Singapore covers an area of about 239 square miles (620 square kilometers). This is about the size of the Isle of Man in the Irish Sea, Bahrain in the Persian Gulf, or Guam in the West Pacific.

What is interesting to note is that if we were to add up the population figures of these three islands, the total would come up to less than a quarter of Singapore's 3.49 million people.

Singapore City, in the southern part of the main island, occu-

The Singapore River, where the early traders came. This photograph was taken a number of years ago. Although the barges no longer moor there, it is still the heart of Singapore's business and administrative area.

pies an area of about 38 square miles (98 square kilometers). Not far from it, and sheltered by the island of Sentosa, lies Singapore's natural, deepwater harbor.

Most of the island of Singapore is flat. There is a central hilly region but the highest point, Bukit Timah (*Bukit* is Malay for hill), reaches only a height of about 541 feet (165 meters).

Singapore's three main reservoirs—Seletar, Peirce and MacRitchie—are found in the water catchment area in the center of the island. In recent years, more reservoirs have been added. They include the Kranji and Pandan Reservoirs. The water supply, however, is not enough for Singapore's needs and water has

18

to be brought by pipeline from the state of Johor in Peninsular Malaysia.

There are a number of small streams flowing to the coast. The longest, Seletar River or *Sungai Seletar*, is about 9 miles (15 kilometers) long. The most important is Singapore River where the early traders came, first to sell their goods, and later to build their homes. It remains the heart of the business and administrative area to this very day. The business area is on the south bank and the administrative area on the north bank of the river mouth, as planned more than a 160 years ago.

When the first traders came to Singapore, the whole island was covered with thick, tropical rain forest. The muddy coast and tidal creeks were covered with mangrove swamps. Many varieties of tropical evergreen plants and trees could be found. There were also tigers, wild boars, deer, civet cats, monkeys, crocodiles, snakes, and many kinds of lizards, birds, insects, and fish. Today,

A *musang*, or civit cat, in the Singapore Zoological Gardens.

with the development of industrial areas, housing estates, and new towns, much of the primary forest has been cleared. The tigers, wild boars, and deer have since disappeared.

Pockets of the original vegetation can be found in the nature reserves on the island—the Bukit Timah Nature Reserve, MacRitchie Reservoir, Botanic Gardens—and some of the offshore islands. Some of the smaller animals, such as the monkey, squirrel, tree shrew, flying lemur, and civet cat, still exist, although they are rarely seen. Birds are fewer in number and variety. However, snakes thrive in the forest reserves, and there is a great range of insect life.

Although much of the island has been developed, Singapore has not been turned into a concrete jungle. Visitors are often surprised by the greenness of the city-state. Shady trees line the sides of wide, spacious roads and every available plot of land is turned into little parks with trees, shrubs, and flowering plants. Rock gardens, artificial ponds, and waterfalls are artistically included to soften the image of huge blocks of high-rise buildings.

One look at Singapore and the visitor understands why it is called the "Garden City of Asia." Its cleanliness, too, makes it even more attractive. Tree planting and anti-litter campaigns over the years have helped to improve the environment.

But how does Singapore manage to look so green throughout the year? "It's our abundant rainfall," the Singaporeans point out. It certainly is! In Singapore, it is summer all the year round. Tourists en route to the island republic are only too happy to leave their winter clothes behind. But they are warned that umbrellas

A view of the coastline of Singapore from Sentosa Island.

are needed, for the rainfall is heavy. Much of it falls in short, sudden showers. As in most hot and humid equatorial regions, much of the rainfall is convectional—the intense heating of the land causes warm air to rise; when this warm air reaches cooler levels, it condenses to form clouds and then rain.

Singapore is affected by the monsoons, too. These are seasonal winds that blow from the southwest and the northeast during certain months of the year. The Southwest Monsoon blows from May to September and the Northeast Monsoon from November to March.

During the Northeast Monsoon, the months are cooler because of the heavier rainfall. As it blows over the seas and oceans, the Northeast Monsoon picks up moisture, thus bringing rain to

21

Singapore and Malaysia. There is less rainfall during the Southwest Monsoon.

Singapore experiences frequent thunderstorms during the inter-monsoon months of April and May and October and November. Sudden violent storms, known locally as *sumatras*, are also experienced about three or four times a month from April to November. These *sumatras* bring heavy rainfall, strong winds and brief spells of cool weather. They usually occur at night or in the early hours of the morning.

Singapore can be said to have no distinct wet or dry season, as rain falls throughout the year. The average rainfall per month is about seven inches (180 millimeters), except during November and December when the figure rises to about 10 inches (260 millimeters).

The temperatures in Singapore are fairly constant. The daily maximum temperature is about 86 degrees Fahrenheit (31 degrees Celsius) and the minimum about 75 degrees Fahrenheit (24 degrees Celsius). This may be rather hot for visitors from temperate lands, but the heat is not too unbearable. Being a small island, no part of Singapore is far from the sea, and the sky is never clear of clouds. And then, there is always the rain.

Much of Singapore's ancient history is shrouded in mystery, but a few legends, giving us a glimpse of the past, can be found in the *Malay Annals* (*Sejarah Melayu*), one of the earliest and most important books of Malay literature. Believed to have been written in the 16th century, the *Malay Annals* contains stories of princes and princesses, kings and queens, pirates and folk heroes. These stories of magic, treachery and romance, war and peace, like the legends of King Arthur in English literature, include both fact and fantasy.

Earlier written records about Singapore date from the 14th century. A Chinese writer, Wang Ta-yuan, said it was called *Temasek* which means "Sea Town" or port. He wrote of a small community of Chinese traders who lived beside Malay rice farmers in the southern part of the pirate-infested island. He also described a settlement, further inland on a hill, which has been identified as Fort Canning Hill on the north bank of the Singapore River.

How then did *Temasek* come to be known as Singapore? Why Singapore, the Lion City? A strange name indeed, especially as we know there were no lions in Singapore–only tigers!

A legend, often told to schoolchildren and tourists, describes how Singapore got its name. Taken from the *Malay Annals*, the legend tells how Sang Nila Utama, also known as Sri Tri Buana, a prince of Palembang in Sumatra, first saw the stretch of white sand on the island of Temasek. He and his men set sail from the nearby islands they were visiting and headed for Temasek.

A sudden storm arose. To prevent the royal ship from sinking, everything on board was thrown into the sea, until the only heavy thing that remained was the prince's crown. When this was thrown overboard, the storm stopped and the prince and his men landed safely at Telok Blangah in the southern part of Temasek.

Later, when the prince went inland to hunt at Kuala Temasek– the mouth of the Singapore River–he saw a strange beast. On being told it was a lion, he took it as a good omen and decided to

The Merlion statue at the mouth of the Singapore River. The lion is the symbol of welcome to Singapore.

build a city there. He named his new city *Singapura* ("Lion City"). Singapore is the anglicised version of Singapura.

Sang Nila Utama, who became the first king of ancient Singapura, is said to have ruled from 1299 A.D. to 1347 A.D. He and his successors turned the island into a wealthy trading port. This attracted the envy of the expanding empires of Java and Siam (Thailand), and Singapura came under constant attack.

It was actually destroyed at the end of the 14th century. A small number of Malays continued to live on the island, but the city fell into decay and was finally reclaimed by the jungle.

In the 16th century, the Portuguese arrived. They had discovered the route to the East and its rich, spice trade. Their histori-

24

ans wrote about the area, noting the ruins of a once great city in Singapura. Much later, in 1819, the British rediscovered what was left of the ruins when Sir Stamford Raffles of the East India Company landed at the mouth of the Singapore River to set up a trading post.

Stamford Raffles noted in his observations that there were "the lines of the old city and its defenses" as well as "the tombs of the Malay kings" on Fort Canning Hill.

The Singapore Malays of the early 19th century refused to go near this hill which they called *Bukit Larangan* ("Forbidden Hill"). They claimed it was haunted by the ghosts of ancient kings.

Today, tourists are often shown the shrine on the hill, now renamed Fort Canning Park. Some people believe it is the burial place of the city's legendary founder, Sang Nila Utama. Tradition, however, connects the shrine with the last of Singapura's Malay rulers, Sultan Iskandar Shah, also known as Parameswara, who ruled from 1389 A.D. to 1391 A.D.

2

The Story of Modern Singapore

The story of modern Singapore began in 1819. Its founder was Sir Stamford Raffles of the British East India Company.

Today, a statue of Raffles stands at Empress Place, the administrative area on the north bank of the Singapore River, not far from the river mouth. The statue, unveiled in 1887, was brought to its present site in front of the Victoria Theater and Memorial Hall, during the centenary celebration of the founding of Singapore. In recent years, another statue of Raffles has been erected nearby, to mark the probable site of his landing more than one and a half centuries ago. Besides these two statues in Singapore, there is another, not as well-known, in the north aisle of Westminster Abbey in London.

Raffles started work as a clerk with the East India Company (which had been formed in the reign of Queen Elizabeth I). The aim of the Company was to open up trade between England and India, and the spice islands of the East Indies. Most of its trading posts were in India, but it also had two trading settlements along the Strait of Malacca. One was at Penang, an island off the northwest coast of the Malay Peninsula, the other at Bencoolen in Sumatra. Company officials started off as traders but, as each trading post became more prosperous, these officials soon found themselves governing large areas of land.

In the 15th century, the rich spice trade of the East was controlled by the Arabs. Then came the Portuguese who had, by the 16th century, discovered the route to the East. The Dutch followed in their wake in the 17th century. By the 18th century, the English were also involved in the trade of the East.

Raffles, after serving the East India Company for 10 years in London, came out East in 1805. He was sent to Penang to take up the post of assistant secretary to the governor.

When he later became the lieutenant-governor of Bencoolen, Raffles was convinced that a port to the east of the Strait of

The statue of Sir Stamford Raffles at the probable site of his landing in Singapore in 1819.

A portrait of Sir Stamford Raffles, now in Singapore's National Museum.

Malacca would be a great advantage to the British. First, it would add to the Company's settlements. Second, it would increase British dominance of the Strait of Malacca—an important sea lane for ships plying between India and the East Indies as well as China. Third, it would help to break the strong hold the Dutch had in the rich trade of the East with their important settlements at Malacca in the Malay Peninsula and Batavia in Java.

The search in the region for such a port ended on January 29, 1819, when Raffles landed at the mouth of the Singapore River. Realizing the importance of the island's geographical position,

Raffles signed a treaty with the local Malay chieftain, the *Temenggong*, and the ruler of the island, the Sultan of Johor. He set up a trading post at the river mouth and lost no time in having the land cleared, a settlement started, and piracy in the area suppressed. Laws were drawn up and regulations laid down for the trading post in Singapore.

Raffles insisted that Singapore remain a free port "and the trade thereof open to ships and vessels of every nation, free of duty, equally and alike to all." This policy, combined with the island's central position on the east-west trade routes, its natural deepwater harbor and the relative orderliness on the island itself, contributed to Singapore's early success.

People from many lands flocked to Singapore. There were Chinese, Arabs, Malays, Indians, and Europeans. They turned Singapore into a busy trading and distribution center.

Products from the surrounding areas were brought to Singapore to be shipped to India and Europe. Manufactured goods from Europe were, in turn, brought to Singapore for distribution to the East. This buying and selling of goods, known as *entrepôt* trade, brought increasing prosperity to Singapore.

In 1824, the East India Company bought Singapore and all the islands within 10 miles (16 kilometers) of its shores. Singapore's population, consisting of about 150 Malays and sea gypsies (known as *Orang Laut*) and a handful of Chinese pepper and gambier farmers when Raffles first landed, had by now grown to about 11,000. (Gambier is a type of climbing plant from which a vegetable dye is obtained for use in tanning hides.)

29

During this time, too, the British and the Dutch ended their rivalry in the East. In 1824, the Dutch handed Malacca over to the British in exchange for Bencoolen.

Two years later, in 1826, Penang, Malacca, and Singapore became known as the Straits Settlements. For many years they were governed by the East India Company based in India. In 1867, the control of the Straits Settlements passed to the British government and Singapore received its first governor from England.

The coming of the steamship, and the opening of the Suez Canal in 1869, made Singapore an important coaling station for steamers bound for the East. Trade increased.

Singapore also played an important part in the spread of British influence in the states of the Malay Peninsula. With the development of the tin and rubber industries in the Malay states, Singapore became an even more important center of the *entrepôt* trade.

Singapore's population continued to increase. By the mid-1860s there were over 80,000 people, more than half of whom were Chinese. However the mainly male population did not regard Singapore as their home.

By 1880, Singapore had grown from a trading post into a town. Its population continued to increase so that, by 1911, there were more than 250,000 people. They were of different races and religions and spoke many languages and dialects. It was noted that there were, at that time, "48 races speaking 54 languages!"

In the early 20th century, a railway line was built from the

A painting of the Singapore waterfront in 1861.

southern to the northern coast of Singapore. This line was later linked to the railway network on the mainland when the Johor Causeway was completed. The construction of a civil airport was started. A naval base, too, was established in the northern part of the island.

Singapore soon became increasingly important as a British military base. But this did not prevent the island from falling to Japanese forces in 1942, during the Second World War. For three and a half years, Singapore was known as *Syonan* ("Light of the South"). It was a time of hardship and suffering for the people.

When the British forces returned, in September 1945, a British Military Administration was set up to restore order. Seven months later, the Straits Settlements were dissolved. Penang and Malacca joined the nine Malay states to form the Federation of Malaya. Singapore became a separate Crown Colony.

The British were interested in retaining Singapore as a trading and military base. But the war had changed a lot of things. The people wanted more say in the way they were governed. This resulted in Singapore's first elections in 1948 when, for the first time, six elected local members were included in the Legislative Council.

Negotiations for more independence continued throughout the 1950s. Finally, in 1959, after 140 years of British rule, Singapore was given internal self-government. Local-born Lee Kuan Yew, a Cambridge-educated Chinese lawyer, became the first prime minister of Singapore. The population, by that time, had reached 1,250,000.

In 1961, the prime minister of Malaya, Tungku Abdul Rahman, proposed the formation of Malaysia. Two years later, the Federation of Malaysia was formed, to include the 11 states of Malaya, Singapore, Sabah (North Borneo), and Sarawak.

Thus Singapore became an independent state within the Federation of Malaysia. However, differences arose between the Singapore and Malaysian governments. In 1965, Singapore separated from Malaysia to become an independent republic. It took over complete control of its own government, foreign affairs, and defense.

Led by their elected leaders, with Lee Kuan Yew as prime minister, the people of Singapore continued in their efforts to prosper and to build a nation from the multiracial communities that had made Singapore their home. Lee Kuan Yew stepped down as prime minister in 1990 but still has significant influence as a senior minister in the People's Action Party (PAP).

3

Peoples from Many Lands

The composition of the population of Singapore is one of the most fascinating in the world today. It is made up of many races, speaking different dialects and languages, and practicing different religions, cultures, customs, and traditions.

With no natural resources, such as tin or gold or oil, the story of Singapore has been the story of its people—those of its past as well as those of its present. They have been, still are, and will continue to be the life, energy, and motivating force of its success.

Singapore's population has reached the 3.5 million mark. For an island of its size, this means one of the highest population densities in the world.

The majority of the people in Singapore are Chinese. They form 76.4 percent of the population. The Malays come next with 14.9 percent and the Indians (from all parts of the subcontinent, including those from Pakistan, Bangladesh, and Sri Lanka) 6.4 percent. The remaining 2.3 percent are made up of small communities of Europeans (British, Dutch, French, Germans, Americans,

Singaporeans of different races.

Australians), Eurasians or people of mixed European and Asian parentage, Japanese, and Arabs.

About 80 percent of this interesting multiracial mix of people are locally born. But where did their ancestors come from? Why did they come to Singapore? And when did they come?

The immigrant ancestors came to Singapore from China, the Malay Peninsula, Indonesia, India, Britain, America, Europe, and the Middle East. Some came to make their fortunes before retiring to their homeland where they had left their families. Others came to escape the poverty or disorder in their own countries. Many others came to look for work.

Those who made Singapore their home worked hard. So did their children and their children's children. It is their hard work that has turned an unhealthy, swampy, jungle-covered island into a clean, modern, bustling city state.

Of the three main races in Singapore—Chinese, Malay, and Indian—the Malay is indigenous or native to the land. Malay kings once ruled the island. With the news of the British trading post in Singapore, many Malays from the Malay Peninsula came to the island. This first major group of early immigrants included many Indonesians from the neighboring islands in the south.

The early Malay settlers set up their own *kampungs* or villages, mainly along the coast in the southern part of Singapore. Others settled in the area around Arab Street and Kampung Glam, to the north of the Singapore River, with the Arabs and Indonesians. What they had in common was their faith. They were all Muslims.

Because of their similar racial, cultural, and religious backgrounds, the Malays and the Indonesians intermarried quite freely. By 1824, they formed about 60 percent of the population.

The most outstanding feature of the dress of the Malay is the *sarung*. This is a loose, ankle-length skirt neatly folded and tucked securely around the waist. Some women wear the *sarung* with a tight-fitting, long-sleeved blouse called a *kebaya* which is fastened in front by three brooches. Others wear the *baju kurung* which consists of a loose, long-sleeved blouse worn over a *sarung*. Some women wear head scarves while a small number wear a *mini telekung*—the headdress according to the teachings of Islam, the Muslim religion. Some Malay women still dress this way in Singapore today, although Western-style clothes have become very popular.

Malay men wear the *sarung*, too, with a loose shirt or *baju*. The

35

A Malay band escorting a bride and groom to their bridal car.

sarung can be shortened by simply rolling it up at the waist. For more formal occasions, a suit consisting of a *baju* and matching pair of loose trousers is worn. A short, thigh-length *sarung*, locally known as a *kain samping*, is worn over the trousers.

Most Malay men wear shirts and trousers today, but they can still be seen in their traditional dress, especially at weddings and on festive occasions. Headgear has more or less been dispensed with except when the men go to the mosque to pray. Then they wear a cap called a *songkok*. Those who have been on a pilgrimage to Mecca, the holy city of the Muslims, wear a white skullcap.

Malay food is hot, spicy, and delicious. It makes generous use

36

of spices and seasonings such as chilli, cloves, coriander, tamarind, and coconut milk. The food is eaten with helpings of rice.

The best known Malay dish is *satay*. It consists of small, spicy pieces of beef, chicken, or mutton skewered on thin sticks and barbecued over a charcoal fire. When ready, the *satay* is dipped in a sweet, spicy peanut sauce and eaten with cucumbers, onions, and *ketupat*. *Ketupat* is cooked rice wrapped in plaited coconut leaves.

Malay food contains no pork which, like alcohol, is forbidden to all Muslims. Malays usually eat with their fingers but forks and spoons are also used.

As early as the 14th century, some Chinese traders are known to have lived alongside the Malay farmers in the southern part of

Satay (pieces of barbecued meat on skewers) and the traditional accompaniments—**ketupat**, peanut sauce, cucumbers, and onions.

Chinese Singaporeans enjoying a trip to the theater.

Singapore. When Raffles came, he found about 30 Chinese pepper and gambier farmers on the island.

Many Chinese who came with the first major group of Malay
and Indonesian immigrants were from the older settlements of
Penang and Malacca. Others were from the Rhio Islands to the
south of Singapore, Batavia in Java, Bangkok in what is now
Thailand, and other ports of the region where they had settled
earlier.

Some came direct from China. In 1821, the first junk—a flat-bottomed sailing ship—brought immigrants from Amoy in South China. Thus began a long, continuous period of Chinese immigration to Singapore. By 1836, the Chinese population had overtaken that of the Malays. The Chinese became the largest group in the population and have remained so to this very day.

The early Chinese immigrants came without their women. The sea voyage from China was long and difficult; and the men were often in debt because they had borrowed money to pay for the voyage. Many were ill-treated as they worked to pay off their debts.

Most of the Chinese who came to Singapore were from southern China. Each group spoke a different dialect. They were given an area on the south bank of the Singapore River where they built their own Chinatown.

In the early years, the annual number of Chinese immigrants rose and fell. Many returned to their families in China after making their fortunes in Singapore. New ones came to take their place.

In the mid-19th century, as Singapore became more prosperous and as living conditions improved, the first Chinese women arrived. As the Chinese community became more settled, increasing numbers of women came to set up home with their men. Before long, many local-born Chinese and China-born immigrants had settled permanently in Singapore.

Many Chinese men and women in Singapore today wear Western-style clothes. But some Chinese women still wear the traditional Chinese *cheongsam*. This is a figure-hugging dress with a

39

high, stiff collar. It is worn either short for day wear or long for formal evening wear. The *cheongsam* has side-slits to make walking and sitting easier. The *samfoo*, which consists of a blouse with a high collar, worn over a pair of trousers, is no longer in fashion today.

Chinese food is excellent and varied. There are Teochew, Cantonese, and other dishes from southern China as well as Beijing and Hunanese dishes from northern China. In between are the Shanghainese and Sichuan dishes. Westerners are usually more familiar with Cantonese food which consists of dishes such as suckling pig and shark's fin soup.

The staple food of the Chinese is rice but the northern Chinese prefer buns and noodles made of wheat. Chinese food is normally mild, except for Sichuan food that uses a lot of chilis and peppers. The Chinese use chopsticks to eat their food.

A very interesting subgroup among the Chinese in Singapore are the Peranakans or Straits-born Chinese.

As early as the 14th century, the Chinese had settled in Malacca, the oldest town in the Malay Peninsula. Some, while keeping their Chinese customs and traditions, began adopting part of the language and culture of the Malays. Over the years, the blending of the two cultures has resulted in the creation of a new culture. Many descendants of this group of Chinese migrated to Singapore and Penang. They brought with them their new culture, the Peranakan or Straits Chinese culture.

The language and way of life of these men (known as *babas*) and

A street in Singapore's Chinatown before the stall-owners moved into a new shopping complex nearby.

women (known as *nyonyas*) have undergone such a change that they can almost be considered as a different race altogether from the other Chinese.

Traditionally, the nyonyas wear the sarung and kebaya of the Malay women. Their men changed to European dress in the late-19th century. Today's nyonyas, however, prefer Western-style clothes, and the sarung and kebaya of the older generation are slowly disappearing from the local scene.

Peranakan or *nyonya* food, on the other hand, is very popular in

41

Singapore. The food is a combination of Chinese and Malay styles of cooking. The ingredients used make for a very interesting taste. Seasonings are like those of Malay dishes. Pork, which is forbidden to Muslims, is used in Peranakan food. Rice is served with the various dishes.

The Indian immigrants to Singapore came from all parts of India and Sri Lanka. They spoke many different languages, such as Tamil, Malayalam, or Punjabi. They had varying customs and traditions. Some were Hindus while others were Muslims, Sikhs, or Christians.

Raffles had 120 Indian soldiers with him when he landed in Singapore. Later, the British brought in Indian prisoners as well as laborers to work on constructing roads, bridges, railways, gov-

Indian women in their long, graceful *sarees*. Indians make up over 6 percent of Singapore's population.

ernment buildings, and wharves. But this practice was soon stopped.

The Indian immigrants congregated mainly in Tanjong Pagar, near the harbor, and in Serangoon Road, to the north of the Singapore River. Each group had its own style of dressing. Today, although most Indian men wear shirts and trousers, some can still be seen in their traditional dress. Headgear is no longer worn except by the Punjabi Sikh men who wear turbans.

Indian women can still be seen today in their long, graceful sarees. Some Punjabi women wear trousers with tight-fitting knee-length blouses known as *kameeze*. Twined around their shoulders and over their heads is a long veil.

Indian food, both Hindu and Muslim, consists of milder curries from northern India and hotter curries from southern India. Hindu dishes contain neither beef nor pork. Muslim dishes contain no pork.

Well-known northern Indian dishes include *shish kebab* or cubes of mutton cooked on skewers, and chicken *tandoori* in which the chicken is soaked in spices, lime, and yogurt, and baked slowly in a clay oven called a *tandoor*. Well-known southern Indian dishes include a type of pancake called *dosai*, mutton, and fish curry.

Indian dishes are served with rice, different varieties of pancakes, or Indian bread. An Indian bread popular with most Singaporeans is the *prata* made from wheat flour. The dough is deftly spread into a thin layer, folded, and then fried on a round, flat griddle. If the *prata* is filled with minced meat, chopped

43

onions, and egg, it is then called *murtabak*. Both the *prata* and *murtabak* are eaten with curry.

Like the Malays and the Peranakans, the Indians eat with their fingers. In public eating places where finger bowls are not provided, or where soap and water are not readily available, forks and spoons are used.

Besides the Indians, Chinese, and Malays, other smaller groups of people from the West and from the Middle East came to Singapore to seek their fortune. From the West came the British, Dutch, Germans, and other Europeans. From the Middle East came the Arabs, the Jews, and the Armenians, and from Asia came the Japanese and small groups of other people. Each added its own way of life to the colorful and interesting ones already in Singapore. By the end of the 19th century, Singapore had become Asia's most cosmopolitan city.

Raffles had, of course, wanted the settlement to be properly planned from its very beginning. On his final visit to Singapore, in 1822, he appointed a committee to draw up a town plan using areas on the north bank of the Singapore River for government offices and those on the south bank for commercial offices. The different communities were to be allocated different areas on both sides of the river to prevent quarrels breaking out.

Although the business and administrative areas have remained unchanged to the present day, there is no longer any segregation of the different communities of Singapore. Today, all Singaporeans live together as neighbors, although the names

Prata, a type of Indian bread which is eaten with curry.

Chinatown, Arab Street, and Serangoon Road still exist to remind people of their colorful past.

Although influenced by the West, Singaporeans are very proud of their different backgrounds as can be seen in their dress, food, customs, and festivals.

Tourists are often charmed by the range of styles of dress in Singapore. They like the different types of food, too. There is such a great variety of food in Singapore that it is no surprise to find that eating has become a popular pastime. Eating places are always crowded with Singaporeans and tourists eager to sample food rich in variety and flavor. Prices range from cheap, expensive depending on whether the food is served by local coffee

A hawker food center.

shops, hawker food centers, fast-food counters, coffeehouses and pubs, or air-conditioned restaurants.

For those who want to eat them, there are hot dogs and hamburgers available too. Hotels and restaurants also offer French, German, and other European food. In addition, Japanese, Korean, and Thai food are very popular in Singapore.

The drinks, cakes, and desserts served in Singapore are as interesting and as varied as the people who make them. Not to taste them is to miss an experience of a lifetime!

46

4

Living Together

Besides their different backgrounds, dress, and food, what do we know about the people of Singapore and how they live together on this island?

Singaporeans worship many gods. Throughout the island, there are Chinese temples, Muslim mosques, Christian churches, Hindu temples, Jewish synagogues, Sikh temples and many other places of worship. Their buildings are very interesting to look at, as each is so distinctly different from the others.

It is only in Singapore that so many places of worship are concentrated in such a small area. Some are practically next door to each other. But no one objects to this since there is complete freedom of worship in Singapore.

The main religions practiced are Taoism and Buddhism, Islam, Christianity, and Hinduism. About 56 percent of the population are Taoists and Buddhists. It is quite difficult to separate these two religions because many people practice a mixture of both. To this is often added ancestral worship as well as the teachings of wise men like Confucius.

Many Taoists and Buddhists are Chinese. The early Chinese immigrants, happy to arrive safely in Singapore, often burnt joss sticks in gratitude to their patron gods and goddesses. Simple joss houses soon grew into magnificent temples. One of these is the Thian Hock Keng Temple in Telok Ayer Street. It is the oldest Chinese temple in Singapore. First built in 1821, it is dedicated to the goddess Ma Zu Po, the Queen of Heaven and the patron of sailors.

The Muslims, the majority of whom are Malays, form about 16 percent of the population. Their religion, Islam, was brought to Southeast Asia at the end of the 13th century by Arab merchants.

A Taoist priest. Over half of Singapore's population belong to the Taoist and Buddhist religions.

A Singapore Muslim at prayer.

The native population of the lands in which the Arabs traded embraced Arab beliefs and made it a part of their daily lives.

Muslims believe in their god, Allah, in the Prophet Muhammad, in prayer, fasting, the giving of alms, and pilgrimage to Mecca—the holy city. Every Friday, at noon, Muslim men can be seen making their way to the nearest mosque to pray. All mosques are carefully built so that worshipers face Mecca when they pray. Before entering the mosque, each Muslim has to take off his shoes and wash his face, hands, head, ears, and feet. Muslim women do not go to the mosques; they pray at home.

The oldest mosque in Singapore is the Sultan Mosque in Arab Street. It was first built in 1820 by an Arab. In 1925, the old mosque was pulled down to make way for the present mosque. This building, with its golden domes and minarets, was designed by an English firm.

The Christians, mainly Chinese, but including people of other races, form about 10 percent of the population. Their churches— Roman Catholic and Protestant—can be found in every part of the island.

When Singapore was founded in 1819, a missionary from Malacca came to minister to the small community of Catholics. Other Catholic missionaries soon followed, and churches and schools were built for the Chinese, Indian, and English-speaking communities. Today's Catholic churches are open to people of all races and their schools cater to children of all races and religions.

Protestant missionaries arrived several months after the founding of Singapore. Over the years, several different Protestant groups came to the island. By the end of the 19th century, many new churches had been built and several mission schools, especially those of the Methodist Church, had been established.

The Indians are a deeply religious people, whether they are Hindus, Muslims, Christians, or Sikhs.

The Hindu temples in Singapore are very different from Chinese and Sikh temples. Like those in South India, they have an entrance tower called a *gopuram*. This tower is decorated with colorful carvings of figures from Hindu mythology. Inside the temple is a prayer hall and a shrine which contains statues of Hindu gods and goddesses.

The Sri Mariamman Temple in Temple Street is the oldest and

St. Andrew's cathedral, the largest and oldest Anglican church in Singapore.

most important Hindu temple in Singapore. Built right in the middle of Chinatown, it was first started in 1827 as a simple building of wood and *attap* (palm thatch). The present temple, constructed in 1835, is dedicated to a goddess.

The rest of the population of Singapore either belong to small religious groups with their own beliefs and forms of worship, or are agnostics who do not believe in any god.

As religions vary, so do festivals. Singapore has many festivals throughout the year. Each festival has a cultural flavor of its own. It may be celebrated with the singing of hymns, the chanting of prayers, the beating of drums or a colorful procession through the streets.

51

Most of the festivals do not fall on the same date of the Western calendar every year. This is because the festival dates, which may be Chinese, Malay, or Indian in origin, are calculated according to the lunar calendar.

The Chinese have many festivals. The most important is the Chinese or Lunar New Year. It falls in either January or February. At this time, traditional Chinese families have their annual spring cleaning, cake making, reunion dinners, and round after round of visits to relatives and friends. Celebrations last for 15 days, but this is not strictly observed nowadays as people have to go back to work.

The Singaporean Chinese have also simplified celebrations to suit their way of life. With more women going to work, traditional cakes are no longer made at home. Orders are placed with housewives or at cake shops that specialize in New Year cakes. But this is certainly a time for inviting friends and neighbors, of all races, to the house for cakes and drinks. It is a happy time for children and for young, unmarried people for they are given traditional red packets, or *hong bao*, of crisp new dollar notes and shining coins.

During this season, too, there is a colorful *Chingay* procession through the streets. *Chingay* means "a decorated float." In China, in the olden days, decorated floats were carried through the streets during the Lunar New Year to honor the gods and goddesses. Today, in Singapore, this Chinese tradition has developed into a procession of lion and dragon dancers, acrobats, stilt-walkers, fairytale characters, and various national groups that make up the island's population.

A lion dance to celebrate the Lunar New Year.

There are other interesting Chinese festivals like the *Qing Ming* (pronounced *Ching Ming*) Festival, the Festival of the Hungry Ghosts, and the Mooncake or Lantern Festival, to mention just a few.

During Qing Ming, which usually falls in April, visits are made to the graves of ancestors or to the temples where ancestral tablets and urns, containing the ashes of the dead, are kept. Offerings and prayers are made, for filial piety—the sense of gratitude to one's forefathers—is very important to the Chinese.

When August arrives, there is the Festival of the Hungry

Food offerings to pacify restless spirits—a common sight during the Festival of the Hungry Ghosts.

Ghosts. This is the time when spirits are believed to be released from the underworld to roam the earth for one month. During this period, street operas are performed, food offerings made and paper money burnt to pacify these spirits, especially the restless spirits of those who have died and not been given proper burial ceremonies.

There are not as many street operas today as there were in the early days, but many Chinese still continue to pray and make their simple offerings.

The burning of paper money has been a problem for those living in high-rise buildings. It could cause fire damage as well as nuisance from smoke in the atmosphere. This has been solved by setting aside special areas in the neighborhood where it can be

54

done. This is to prevent any inconvenience to people of other races and religions. It also helps to keep the neighborhood clean, since special containers are used in these areas.

Shopkeepers and market stall-holders often get together to organize a food offering to the spirits. Sometimes, there is even a street opera. Some of these occasions can be quite elaborate, especially if generous donors can be found.

The Mooncake or Lantern Festival is celebrated on the 15th day of the eighth moon. This is the time when the moon is believed to be at its brightest and roundest. It falls during the month of September or October.

Mooncakes are eaten at this time. They are round crusts of pastry filled with bean paste and melon or lotus seeds. Throughout the island, there are competitions for the best-made lanterns, the most original lanterns and so on. At night, Chinese children carry lighted lanterns of every shape and color. Malay, Indian, European children, and children of other races, too, join in the fun.

Some people claim that the Mooncake Festival is celebrated to commemorate the victory of the Chinese people over the Mongols during the Ming Dynasty. Messages hidden inside mooncakes and lanterns were said to have signaled the start of the rebellion in ancient China.

There is another interesting Chinese story that is often told in connection with the Mooncake Festival. It is about a cruel king who discovered a drink that would make him immortal. For the sake of the people, the queen decided to destroy it. But she was caught in the act. To avoid punishment, she swallowed the drink and made a leap for freedom. She landed on the moon and is believed to live there still. The Mooncake Festival is said to be celebrated in her honor.

The two main Malay festivals are Hari Raya Puasa and Hari Raya Haji. Hari Raya Puasa marks the end of the Muslim fasting, or *puasa*, month of Ramadan. It usually falls during August.

The occasion begins with the sighting of the new moon. The next morning, thanksgiving prayers are offered in mosques throughout the island. Then comes the feasting and the visits to relatives and friends. Like the Chinese New Year, it is a time of celebration. Friends and neighbors of all races are invited home to a delicious feast of Malay food, cakes, and drinks.

Hari Raya Haji is celebrated in October to mark the end of the annual pilgrimage to the holy city of Mecca in Saudi Arabia. To the Muslims, this is a time for giving alms to the poor, renewing friendships, patching up quarrels, and granting forgiveness.

The Indians, especially the Hindus, have many festivals. Two of them are Thaipusam and Deepavali.

Thaipusam is a religious festival. It celebrates the victory of the Hindu god, Lord Subramaniam, over a demon. Lord Subramaniam's image is carried on a lighted chariot from one main Hindu temple to another. There is also a procession of *kavadi* bearers. *Kavadis* are metal or wooden arches, some studded with sharp spikes and skewers. They are carried on the shoulders of Hindus who want to fulfil vows of thanksgiving or those who want to punish themselves for the wrong they have done.

56

Deepavali, which means "a row of lights," is celebrated in either October or November. It is an occasion for much rejoicing for it celebrates the triumph of light over darkness, or good over evil.

On the eve of the festival, colored lamps, candles, and rows of oil lamps are lighted in all Hindu homes. The next morning, the Hindus go to the temples to pray. Later in the day, visitors are received at home and entertained with special cakes made for the occasion. Younger members of the family go out to visit relatives and friends. The ladies are in their most beautiful *sarees*, some with flowers in their long, black, neatly plaited hair. Younger girls wear their traditional short blouses and long, colorful skirts.

A *kavadi* bearer at the Hindu festival of *Thaipusam*.

A spice shop in Serangoon Road, Singapore's "Little India."

Several days before Deepavali, Thaipusam, and other festive occasions, Serangoon Road is full of shoppers. This area, known as Singapore's "Little India," sells anything from flowers and *sarees* to spices needed for Indian cooking. Everything an Indian needs for his religious ceremonies, his wedding, or other festive occasions, can be found in the shops along this road. It is a popular place with Singaporeans and tourists who come to the area to shop, see another way of life, and eat at the many Indian restaurants.

The Christians of Singapore have their Good Friday services and Easter celebrations to mark the death and resurrection of

Christ as well as the celebration of Christmas with Christmas trees, lights, and carols.

Shops and department stores all over Singapore are lighted up weeks before Christmas. Everyone shops for presents, even non-Christians. No matter what their race or religion, everyone has presents to buy for friends who celebrate Christmas.

There are so many festivals in Singapore that only seven have been declared public holidays. Besides these seven, there are three other public holidays—New Year's Day (January 1), Labor Day (May 1), and National Day (August 9).

National Day, of course, marks the day when Singapore became an independent nation. It is celebrated with a parade at the Padang, the field in front of the City Hall.

Festivals are enjoyed by everyone in Singapore. Many, though, are not celebrated as elaborately as in the past. This is because customs have been simplified to suit the changing pace of modern living. Celebrations continue, nevertheless, providing families, relatives, and friends of all races with time to get together to eat, talk, and laugh. When the celebrations are over and it is time to go home, many head for their high-rise housing estates and new towns in different parts of the island.

In the early days when the population increased rapidly through immigration, there were not enough houses for the people. The city became overcrowded. Many families lived in slums and in roughly built houses in squatter areas.

As early as 1927, the Singapore Improvement Trust was set up to tackle the problems of housing. In 32 years it provided 23,000

National Day celebrations in front of the City Hall, to mark the anniversary of Singapore's independence.

homes in the housing estates of Tiong Bahru, Kallang, and part of Queenstown.

In 1960, a year after Singapore achieved internal self-government, a Housing and Development Board was set up to tackle the housing problem. In its first five-year program, from 1960 to 1965, the board built 54,000 housing units. From then on, until 1980, the board built a total of 370,000 housing units.

Singapore's building program has been so successful that almost 80 percent of the population now live in modern, low-cost apartments. In the 1990s, the board built many new towns and housing estates in various parts of the island.

High-rise buildings and skyscrapers are a common sight in Singapore because there is not enough land to build on. This shortage of land, unfortunately, has led to the pulling down of old bungalows and two-story shops characteristic of Singapore's earlier period. In recent years, however, more has been done than in the past to preserve existing old buildings as part of the nation's heritage. The people have adapted well to high-rise living; and easy, long-term payments have encouraged many to buy their own Housing and Development Board homes. There are homes that the middle and lower income groups can afford to buy as well as those for the middle to upper income groups.

New towns and housing estates in Singapore are well-designed and landscaped. They are also self-sufficient, each with shops, markets, schools, and community facilities, such as playgrounds, swimming pools, sports centers, libraries, theaters, and community centers.

Besides public housing, there are also homes built privately for those who can afford them, including blocks of apartments with their own property management to look after the landscaped gardens, swimming pools, squash and tennis courts.

Singaporeans of all races live as neighbors in these homes now. Living together was not easy at first. But, over the years, the different races have learned to be more understanding and tolerant. Many have become friends. So have their children, who play together and go to school together.

Children from different racial groups prepare to present a song and dance routine at a school concert.

Schools throughout the island, whether they are government or mission (government-aided) schools, take in children of all races and religions. Like children in Britain and the United States, the children in Singapore learn to read and write and do arithmetic. As they grow older, they study science, history, geography, and other subjects.

English-medium schools, where all teaching is in English, are very popular in Singapore. Most parents send their children to these schools because English is useful in the learning of science and technology. It is also the language used in administration and in institutions of higher learning.

But we must not forget that Singapore is a multiracial country. So all the children have to learn two languages—English, and either Malay (the national language), Chinese (Mandarin), or Tamil.

Primary education, which begins at the age of six, is free but not compulsory. It can be completed in six or eight years according to the children's capability. In the first few years, emphasis is on language learning. Children who cannot manage two languages are streamed into classes where only one language is taught.

Those who pass the Primary School Leaving Examination go on to secondary schools. There, they do a four- or five-year course before taking their Singapore-Cambridge "O" (Ordinary) level examination. Fees for secondary schools are nominal.

Vocational and industrial training is also available. So is technical education. There are commercial classes, and two- or three-year pre-university classes in schools and junior colleges for those who are likely to be accepted at a university.

State assistance is given to pupils who cannot afford to pay fees or buy textbooks. Scholarships, bursaries, and study loans are also offered. There is equal opportunity for every pupil no matter what his or her race, religion, or family background.

All schools follow a common, local syllabus. Moral education is considered an important part of a child's education. So is physical and social development. Schools plan their own extracurricular activities, such as sports, games, debating societies, scouting and girl guide movements, bands, and so on.

Schools in Singapore operate in two sessions—one in the morning and the other in the afternoon. Pupils attend either one or the other. This is because of the large number of children of school age. There are, however, enough places for all those who need them.

Classes, which tended to be rather large with about 40 to 44 children per class, have gradually become smaller. This is due to the successful family planning program introduced by the government in 1966, to reduce the birthrate.

Since 1970, the Ministry of Culture has been promoting the art, music, dance, and drama of the various races in Singapore. Regular exhibitions, concerts, and stage performances are organized. Cultural performances are also shown on television. All these have helped to make Singaporeans familiar with one another's culture.

Singapore's dance groups are sent to perform in countries all over the world. They have appeared in countries as far apart as Australia, South Korea, Belgium, and America. Foreign artists, too, are invited to perform in Singapore.

Chinese, Malay, Indian, and Western music each have their own charm. The movements of dancers and the rich, colorful costumes worn by each group have a distinctive beauty. Photographs may give an idea of the different dances performed in Singapore but they cannot convey the music and movements that go with each dance. Televised performances are better but nothing can take the place of the thrill, sight and sound of an actual performance!

A Chinese opera performance, showing characters in their traditional colorful costumes.

Today, Singapore has its own symphony orchestra. It also holds a festival of arts once every two years. This has not only aroused a lot of interest in the local arts among the general public but has also attracted artists from other countries.

Interest has also been shown in painting, sculpture, photography, poetry, song writing, story writing, and plays. Competitions are held regularly to encourage greater participation.

Children, especially, are encouraged to read more. Singapore's National Library has over a million books in Malay, Chinese, Tamil, and English for adults and children. To cater for the needs of the reading public, it has branch libraries in different parts of the island.

What about sports in Singapore? Almost every game, from soccer and basketball to golf, badminton, squash, and windsurfing, is enjoyed by Singaporeans. There are many sports facilities on the island. Some are privately run while others are open to the public. The most popular sports in Singapore are jogging, swimming, and soccer.

Several parks and offshore islands have been developed as recreation areas. People can relax here in quiet, beautiful surroundings away from the hustle and bustle of city life. A favorite spot is the East Coast Park where the public can cycle, jog, swim, picnic or hold barbecue parties. The park also has a "fit-

Sentosa Island, a popular vacation resort to the south of Singapore, which certainly lives up to the meaning of its name—Isle of Peace and Tranquility.

ness corner" where people do exercises to keep themselves physically fit.

Another favorite spot is Sentosa Island to the south of Singapore. Formerly used as a British fortress and military base, this offshore island has been developed into a vacation resort for Singaporeans and tourists. From Pulau Blakang Mati, its name has been changed to Pulau Sentosa ("The Isle of Peace and Tranquillity").

Vacationers can take a ferry to the island or they can go by cable car. There are many sports facilities on the island. These include the bicycle and pony-riding tracks, the golf course, and areas for swimming, canoeing, and windsurfing. There is even a place where the young can roller skate or dance if they want to. Other attractions include a monorail, a musical fountain, a food center, an art center, several museums, and a coralarium where seashells, corals, and marine life associated with coral reefs are on display. There is also a hotel for tourists and a camp for youngsters who want to experience outdoor living.

Other offshore islands, too, have been developed and are very popular with picnickers and those interested in fishing, snorkelling, and scuba diving.

Schoolchildren have their own sports, games, and other activities. Those who attend the morning sessions at school have their activities in the afternoon. Those who go to school in the afternoon take part in other activities in the morning.

When there are no planned activities in school, the children go to playgrounds or libraries near their homes. Some prefer to stay

One of the many public swimming pools built in housing estates throughout the island.

at home to study, listen to the radio, or watch television. Others go to nearby parks to fly kites or cycle with their friends. There are also community centers where they can play basketball or badminton, and swimming pools where they can swim or play water polo.

During long school holidays in June and December, young people go camping at the beach or at some of the offshore islands. Some, whose parents can afford it, go traveling. They visit Malaysia and other Asian countries, Australia, Europe, or the United States. Other young people spend their vacations working at fast-food counters or in department stores all over Singapore.

Although Singaporeans do not have mountains to climb or much countryside to explore, there are many other things they can do. Concerts, dance performances, plays, and exhibitions attract large crowds of people. So do the beaches, parks, cinemas, modern shopping complexes, restaurants, and food centers.

5

Earning a Living

For over a century, *entrepôt* trade was the most important force in Singapore's economy. As a commercial center for import and export, it provided thousands of jobs. This trade also helped Singapore grow from a fishing village into a modern city-state.

Singapore's geographical position made it an ideal collecting and distribution center for the region. From spices in the early days, the trade shifted to sugar, coffee, and copra (dried coconut kernels). Later, there was tin, rubber, crude oil, and manufactured goods from the East.

Today, Singapore trades with almost all nations in the world. Its main trading partners are Malaysia, Japan, the United States, Saudi Arabia, and the European Union. These countries make up about two-thirds of the island's total trade. Crude oil, electronic parts, iron and steel, and aircraft and ships are imported into Singapore. The island's main exports include petroleum products, machinery and equipment, electronic products, and crude rubber.

No country, however, can depend on trade alone. It has to develop in other directions as well. Over the years, the other ports in the region had been offering stiffer competition for the trade in the area. And, with declining trade, Singapore had to make other plans.

The population in Singapore had also increased rapidly. The increase, especially in the years after the Second World War, was a world record! As a result, besides housing, education, better health and medical services for the people, more jobs were urgently needed. Since agriculture was out of the question because of the shortage of land, and it was not possible to expand the *entrepôt* trade, attention was directed toward industrialization instead.

Before 1961, industry in Singapore was limited to the processing of rubber and copra, tin smelting, and the refining of vegetable and coconut oils. Other light industries included the manufacture of furniture, footwear, clothes, food, and bottled drinks for the home market.

The industrialization program was introduced in the early 1960s. The government spent millions of dollars to turn Jurong—a swamp in the southwestern part of the island—into an industrial area. Hills were leveled, swamps filled, and roads and factories built. This was followed up by the construction of high-rise homes for the workers and their families. Markets, schools, landscaped parks, and other recreational facilities were also provided.

Industries set up in the area included shipbuilding and repairing yards, car assembly plants, and petroleum refineries as well as factories producing everything from plywood, plastics, ceramics, steel tubes, and tires to electrical and electronic goods.

Many conditions were just right for the new industrialization in the 60s. Communications facilities were well-developed. So was the water and electricity supply. The port, banks, and other services were all ready to serve the needs of the manufacturing industries. Singapore also had a stable government and a large pool of skilled labor.

As a result, many local and foreign investors set up industries in Singapore. They were given every encouragement, including attractive tax incentives. The industrial drive was so successful that manufacturing became a major contributor to Singapore's economy. For the first time in history, Singapore was no longer totally dependent on entrepôt trade.

When there was not enough land available in Jurong for more factories, smaller industrial estates were started in different parts of the island. Today, Singapore has 30 industrial estates of which Jurong is the largest. All are managed by the Jurong Town Corporation, which was set up in 1968. There are altogether slightly less than 5,000 companies.

With full employment achieved in the early 1970s, Singapore has turned its attention to higher technology industries. It is also moved toward mechanization, computerization, and the increasing use of industrial robots. Next to Japan, Singapore is Southeast Asia's second largest user of robots in factories.

The very success of Singapore's industrialization program has also led to its growth in trade, port services, transportation, and communications, banking and finance, and construction and tourism.

72

A view of the Singapore River before 1983 when the barges were restricted to the Pasir Panjang Wharves.

The port of Singapore is one of the busiest in the world. Ships of more than 500 shipping lines, from many countries, use its excellent facilities. Every day, there are more than 600 ships in Singapore—from lighters, trawlers and coastal vessels to super-tankers, container ships, cargo freighters, bulk carriers, and passenger vessels.

The port is run by the Port of Singapore Authority. It operates five gateways: Keppel Wharves, the Tanjong Pagar Container Terminal, Pasir Panjang Wharves, and Jurong Port—all in the southern part of the island—and Sembawang Wharves in the north.

Increasing use is made of the Tanjong Pagar Container Terminal, which started operations in 1972. Extension work is

73

being carried out to enable more containerized cargo from all parts of the world to be handled at the terminal. Other types of cargo are unloaded or loaded at the wharves. Lighters (boats used for shifting goods between ship and land) are also used.

The port of Singapore operates round-the-clock throughout the year. It provides every service that is related to shipping. The people who work there include harbor pilots, customs officers, stevedores, mechanics, technicians, policemen, firemen, engineers, administrators, office staff, and other personnel.

Many other people earn their living in the transportation and communications sector. Since the days of Raffles, transportation has progressed from the sailing ship to the steamship, the car, the train, and the airplane. Today, with links to most countries in the world by radio, submarine cables, computers, and satellites, Singapore has become an important telecommunications center for Asia.

Singapore has an efficient postal service and an up-to-date telephone service for local and international calls. There are modern facilities for telegrams, photo-telegrams, faxes, and overseas computer links. Singapore is also an important relay center for air and sea communications and meteorological information.

An excellent network of roads and expressways links the island from end to end. A rail-based subway Mass Rapid Transit system (MRT) provides fast and efficient transportation for thousands along its two lines.

The island has a railway line offering passenger services from Tanjong Pagar in the southern part of Singapore to the Johor

Bridges and expressways such as these link the island from end to end.

Causeway in the north. It is connected to the railway network in Peninsular Malaysia. Bus drivers, taxi drivers, railway workers, postmen, telephone operators, radio and computer personnel are some of the people working in the transportation and communications sector.

Air transportation has also provided work for the people of Singapore. Being central to international air routes, Singapore has become an important servicing center in Southeast Asia. As a result, more planes fly in and out of Singapore; and the Singapore Changi Airport, opened in July 1981, has enjoyed both passenger and freight increase. Further expansion has been carried out to meet the growth of air traffic in the last decade.

The developed air, sea, rail, and road communications have

75

given rise to tourism. To cater to the increasing number of tourists
visiting Singapore, hotels have been built. So have shopping complexes, restaurants, and many recreational facilities.

In recent years, tourism has made a significant contribution to
Singapore's economy. The tourist industry, vigorously promoted

and developed by the Singapore Tourist Promotion Board, has attracted many visitors to the island republic. From mere thousands in the early sixties, tourist arrivals in the past few years have reached almost three million per year. Most of the tourists come from neighboring countries in Southeast Asia, and from Japan, Australia, New Zealand, India, Europe, Canada, and the United States.

Why do tourists come to Singapore? There are few places of historical interest, few natural beauty spots. Yet the island seems to have a fascination for people from near and far.

Those from Malaysia, Indonesia, Thailand, the Philippines, and India come mainly to shop for duty-free goods, such as radios, cameras, television sets, cosmetics, curios, clocks and watches. Shops and department stores are well-stocked with goods from all over the world. Most of the shops, together with the island's best and biggest hotels, are concentrated in Orchard Road, Singapore's main tourist district.

Tourists from Australia, New Zealand and countries in the West, come to shop, to enjoy the food, and see the fascinating variety of religions, cultures, customs, and traditions of the different races in Singapore.

The republic is also one of the safest cities in the world. It is clean and green and there is a wide choice of comfortable and well-run hotels. Postal, telephone, and other services are excellent and tourists are delighted to find that everything works in Singapore.

All this has meant more jobs for the people of Singapore,

because hotel personnel, sales personnel, tour guides, tour operators and others are needed to keep the tourist industry going.

Many other people work in banks and finance companies which have branches throughout the island. Trade, manufacturing, and foreign investment have all given rise to a great variety of banking and financial services. As a result, Singapore has developed into a banking and financial center for the region.

At the end of 1990, there were over 100 banks in Singapore. A few were local banks while most were foreign banks. Singapore's Shenton Way, where most of the banks are sited, is the equivalent of New York's Wall Street.

The banks, most of which are computerized, employ large numbers of people. Others work in the finance companies and insurance companies, and the many financial institutions set up to deal with the foreign exchange market as well as the Asian dollar market.

Other Singaporeans earn their living in the construction industry. In the past 40 years, much land has been cleared and construction projects have been carried out in various parts of the island. Homes were needed. So were schools, factories, recreational centers, and hotels.

Roads have been constantly improved and expressways have been built. The size of the island was also increased by nearly a tenth through the reclamation of land from the sea. All these projects have meant more jobs for the people of Singapore.

As the construction industry continued to grow, shortage of labor became a problem. Foreign "guest" workers had to be

Part of the business district of Singapore.

employed—from Malaysia, Indonesia, India, South Korea, Macau, and the Philippines. They, however, have mostly been phased out in the 1990s, for the government believes that Singapore should not depend too much on foreign labor.

Some people in Singapore run their own family businesses. These may be small provision shops, noodle factories, import and export firms, or food stalls and restaurants.

An automatic poultry-feeding system at the Primary Production Department's experimental station.

A small number of people earn their living through farming. As land is scarce, most farms in Singapore are very small. The traditional method of mixed farming has now given way to intensive farming. Because of this, Singapore is able to produce enough eggs, poultry, and pork for its people.

Market gardens grow about one-quarter of the fresh vegetables needed for local consumption. The rest of the vegetables are imported, mainly from neighboring Peninsular Malaysia. Fruits are also grown and mushrooms cultivated for the home market. Orchids, for which Singapore is well-known, are grown for export.

About 6 percent of the total land area of Singapore is used for

An orchid farm in Singapore's Botanical Gardens. Many orchids are grown for export in Singapore.

agriculture. Farms and farming land will continue to decrease because of resettlement due to housing and industrial development. But there are plans to set aside certain rural areas for long-term intensive farming.

Singapore's fishermen catch about a quarter of the fish eaten locally. The fish is caught in the Indian Ocean, in the South China Sea, and in the surrounding waters. In addition, fish breeding is carried out in fish ponds. Prawns and certain other types of shellfish are also bred.

Not all fish are eaten, however. Some, like the beautiful and colorful aquarium fish, are sold to the local public as well as to overseas buyers. There is a growing market for these aquarium fish.

To help local farmers and fishermen, the Primary Production Department carries out research and provides services in all areas of agricultural activity.

6

Building a Nation

The island of Singapore has changed beyond recognition since it became a fully independent republic in 1965. The most dynamic changes have been in the economy. It is easy to see how prosperous Singapore has become. The people enjoy full employment, rising incomes, and better housing; their children get equal opportunities in education; the city-state is clean and beautiful, and public services are excellent.

Compared with their immigrant forefathers, the people of today are more disciplined, more united, more proud of themselves and their young nation. They work, play, and progress together and are very tolerant of one another's beliefs and customs. Nowhere in the world is there a better example of harmony among so many different races.

How did this come about? Since Singapore is multiracial, multilingual, multi-religious, and multicultural, it was indeed difficult to believe that the people of Singapore could become one nation.

The City Hall, with the dome of the Supreme Court in the background.

They had nothing in common—no shared history, no similar language, no common culture, no single religion.

But they were a hard-working population. Credit must certainly go to the people of different races who have made Singapore what it is today. A stable, progressive government has been able to steer the nation toward economic success.

Singapore has been fortunate in having a continuous leader-

84

ship. As the elected government, Singapore's leaders have been in office much longer than many famous leaders in the world today. The present ruling party is the People's Action Party (PAP). It won all seats in six general elections held since 1959. In the seventh general election held in December 1984, it won an overwhelming 77 out of a total of 79 seats.

By 1997 PAP still held all but a few of the seats in parliament. Singapore is a republic with a parliamentary system of government. Parliament has a life span of five years. General elections are held within three months after each parliament is dissolved. Voting is compulsory for every citizen age 21 and over.

Today's parliament is made up of 83 elected members, from each constituency in Singapore. Parliament elects the president—the head of state of the nation—for a term of six years. The president, in turn, appoints the prime minister—the member who has the confidence of the majority in parliament. He also appoints the cabinet of 14 ministers on the advice of the prime minister.

The rules of procedure in parliament are adapted from those of the British House of Commons at Westminster. Since Singapore has four official languages—Malay (the national language), Chinese (Mandarin), Tamil and English—members of parliament can use any official language in debates. Simultaneous translation is provided.

When Singapore started as a young, new republic, it had a Malay president, a Chinese prime minister, and an Indian foreign minister. This racial mix is seen not only in the government but everywhere else in Singapore.

The Singapore national flag.

All citizens enjoy equal opportunities in education, housing, employment, and health services. There is no segregation in schools, offices, factories, shops, or buses, and no special privileges for any class of people. Recruitment for jobs is based on aptitude, ability, and merit. So are promotions.

In the early 1960s, more than half the population was under 20 years of age. This meant that more schools had to be built during this period, with each school having two sessions.

Children attend Chinese, Malay, Tamil, or English-medium

schools. All learn a second language. This is usually English in the Chinese, Malay, and Tamil-medium schools. Children in an English-medium school learn Chinese, Malay, or Tamil (depending on their mother tongue), as their second language.

All four language streams are given equal treatment. Before each school session, children sing the national anthem *Majulah Singapura* ("Let Singapore Flourish") in Malay, the national language. They are also introduced to Singapore's red and white flag with its white crescent moon and five white stars. The coat of arms is a shield supported on the left by a lion and on the right by a tiger.

Children of all races work and play together. They have a common, neutral language in which to communicate—English. They study the same lessons, learn common values, and share common interests. They learn to become Singaporeans.

As Singapore's economy expanded from its traditional *entrepôt* trade into industrialization, changes were made in the education system. Besides academic studies, there is also technical, industrial, and vocational training.

Through the years, education has not only kept pace with the demands of Singapore's changing economy, but with parents' preferences as well. Today, more and more parents want their children to learn English. Changes have been made and will continue to be made to further improve the education system of Singapore.

About 91 percent of the present population of Singapore are literate compared to about 52 percent in the 1950s. The total num-

The old and new faces of Singapore—a modern housing development towering above old houses and shops in Chinatown.

ber of students in the National University of Singapore, the Nanyang Technological Institute, the Singapore Polytechnic, Ngee Ann Polytechnic, and the Institute of Education, has also increased. There are 10 times more students in these tertiary institutions today than there were in 1959. Many more people, too, can speak and write at least two languages—their mother tongue and English.

Singapore's rapid industrialization threw workers of all races together. So did the government's housing program. Many people had to learn new skills. They also had to learn to adapt themselves to high-rise living.

88

The stress of modernization was greater for older people and those who had to be resettled because of these new developments. It was especially difficult for the people used to the more leisurely pace of life in the small *kampungs* or villages that they had to leave.

Many problems had to be overcome during the years, but as everyone was in the same boat, the Malays, Chinese, Indians, Eurasians, and other races learned to live and work together.

Community centers, built mainly in public housing estates, also helped to play a part in nation building. They brought people of all races together. They helped to promote neighborliness through cultural activities, educational classes, sports, and social get-togethers.

In the early days, community centers were single-story buildings made of wood and zinc. They were simply furnished. A single room often served as an office, a games room, and a classroom. The main activities organized were usually sewing classes for the girls and games like table tennis, Chinese chess, and basketball for the boys. The people who usually went to these community centers were the Chinese-educated.

In the 1960s, as factories and homes mushroomed in different parts of the island, concrete-built community centers were erected in the midst of the housing estates. These centers provided some breathing space for the people living in high-rise buildings.

As Singapore became more prosperous, better community centers were built. Designs for each became more individual to create a sense of identity. Each had squash and tennis courts, ballet and music rooms, audiovisual rooms, large reception halls, and other rooms designed for the many courses conducted in the centers. A wide range of courses is offered—from cooking, fashion designing, aero-modeling, stilt-walking, and computer programming to music, languages, photography, and Eastern and Western dancing. Fees are kept low so that everyone can afford to attend the classes.

Today's activities are organized for the entire family, including kindergarten classes, indoor and outdoor games, and senior citizens' clubs for the elderly. Educational tours are conducted, concerts planned, and trips to places of interest organized.

Singaporeans of all races make use of the community centers built in constituencies throughout the island. They come from all walks of life to share the many opportunities for meeting people and making friends.

Chinese children at a community center kindergarten class.

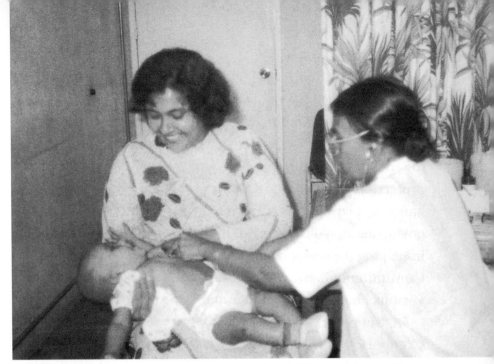

A maternal and childcare clinic—an example of Singapore's excellent medical facilities.

In building a nation, the health of the people is of great importance. With good housing, modern sanitation, and the rising standard of living, the people's health has progressively improved.

Today, in Singapore, the streets and drains are clean. Tap water is perfectly safe for drinking, and major diseases like tuberculosis and smallpox are no longer common. There are few cases of infant deaths and people generally live longer. Health care for the public is provided through outpatient clinics, school health services, and maternal and childcare centers. There are dental services and public as well as private hospitals for the sick.

Medical and health services have to be paid for but public

health services, subsidized by the government, are much cheaper than private ones. Free services are given only to citizens too poor to pay for them.

Singapore also has social welfare services that help the aged, the destitute, and children and young people in need of protection. In addition, help is given to the needy, the handicapped, and victims of floods and fires. Besides the government, voluntary welfare organizations also play a part in helping the less fortunate. Singaporeans donate money to a fund that has been set up to support the various charitable organizations.

In Singapore, people who work are encouraged to save. Compulsory contributions are made by both workers and employers to the Central Provident Fund. This form of saving is to ensure that workers are provided for in their old age or when they are unfit to work. Workers can use these savings to pay for their homes or their medical expenses.

The government has also set up the Singapore Family Planning and Population Board to make the people more aware of the disadvantages of having too many children. Campaigns for the two-child family have resulted in a drop in the rate of population growth in the republic.

As a new nation, Singapore needed its own military forces. With the withdrawal of British troops from the bases on the island, it became necessary to call up and train soldiers as quickly as possible. In 1967, compulsory national service was introduced for all young, able-bodied male citizens when they reached the age of 18.

A training exercise for Singapore's national servicemen.

The republic knows that it is too small to be a threat to any nation. It also knows that its small size can be a disadvantage. So it is prepared to protect its own property and to defend its way of life. The young men in Singapore's armed forces—the army, the navy, and the air force—are trained to be ready and able to defend the island. Singapore's armed forces, like those of Switzerland, are based on the citizen soldier. Each young man is given two to two and a half years of military training to enable him to help defend his country. After his training, he returns to civilian life—to his university studies or his job. He then attends regular training sessions each year and remains in reserve for 10 years or until he is 40 years of age. Those who are interested in a military career can sign up as regulars in the army, navy, or air force.

During national service, young men of all races train together. Military units are a complete racial mix. Everyone shares the same tough training. The young men share the fun of living, too. They share common values, develop similar attitudes, and build up a sense of belonging.

It is interesting to see how Singapore has developed into a single nation with the Chinese, the Malays, the Indians, the Eurasians, and all the other races thinking of themselves as Singaporeans first. They are as completely Singaporean as the diverse peoples of the United States are wholly and completely American.

Singaporeans remain proud of their own heritage, but this has not prevented them from absorbing some parts of the culture of the other races. This has happened because of years of constant contact with one another. This interesting and unique blending of four great cultures—Chinese, Malay, Indian, and Western—can be seen in Singapore today, especially in the people's art, music, dance, cooking, and dress.

7

Looking Ahead

When Singapore became an independent republic there were many tasks to be done, challenges to be met and problems to be solved.

The older generation who have lived through the early years of independence ,remember them as a time of uncertainty and discontent. Singapore's present success has come only after years of hard work and sacrifice. But now these efforts have been rewarded. The people have learned to live and work together as one nation. Their children have grown up to identify themselves as Singaporeans. They have progressed and they have become prosperous.

What of the place Singapore has carved for itself in the world and the preparations it is making for the future?

As early as 1967, Singapore had become a member of the Association of Southeast Asian Nations (ASEAN) together with Malaysia, Thailand, Indonesia, and the Philippines. Since then, these five nations have been working to strengthen their econom-

The Singapore Conference Hall, the venue for many national and international conferences and meetings.

ic, technical, and cultural ties. They cooperate with one another to achieve progress and stability in the region. Brunei joined this group of nations in 1984 and Vietnam became a member in 1995.

Besides cooperating with its neighbors, Singapore has friendly ties with many countries throughout the world. It has a great number of embassies, high commissions, and other diplomatic missions abroad. And many countries, in their turn have representatives in Singapore.

Singapore's leaders take part in regional and international conferences and meetings. They visit countries at the invitation of friendly governments. Ministers and representatives of nations from all over the world also visit Singapore to discuss trade, ship-

96

The World Trade Center. Singapore now trades with many countries throughout the world.

ping, civil aviation, and other matters. There is a continuous exchange of views, and much planning for cooperation in science, technology, and industry.

Developed countries, like Japan, France, and Germany, have given Singapore technical assistance. They have helped to set up training centers on the island where their experts teach technical skills to workers. Equipment and training awards are generously provided. In turn, Singapore helps its fellow developing nations in the region in fields like engineering, housing development, park development, port activities, and communications.

As a member of the United Nations Organization, Singapore plays an active role in promoting peace and cooperation among

97

The modern skyline of Singapore—the city-state which has come a long way since Sir Stamford Raffles first landed there in 1819.

nations. It is involved in many of the United Nation's international agencies.

As an independent nation and an *entrepôt* center, Singapore trades with countries all over the world, even those with different types of government. It respects the right of other countries to determine their own future and expects the same respect for its right to map out its own destiny.

In 1985, Singapore was rated as the country with the most outstanding export growth and the country with the fastest growing economy in the world. Still, the people are constantly urged to keep up their good work. Great emphasis is placed on skill training and productivity, for Singapore is aware that everything the people have worked for can just as easily disappear if considerable effort is not made to keep up with modern technology.

Future oil crises, a drop in international trade, developments in other parts of the world, and instability in neighboring countries will always have an effect on Singapore's economy. Other problems will include competition from newly developing countries, changes in the world markets, or even the rise and fall of the currencies of different countries.

No one can foretell what the future will bring, but with peace and stability in the region, Singapore can face its future with confidence. It can continue to encourage individuals in each sector to learn the higher skills that are so necessary to the republic as it moves on to the 21st century.

GLOSSARY

chingay	Decorated float
Deepavali	Hindi festival celebrating triumph of light over darkness
filial piety	The sense of gratitude to one's forefathers
gambier	Climbing plant from which vegetable dye is taken and used for tanning hides
joss stick	Slender stick of incense
kampungs	Villages
kebaya	Long-sleeved, tight-fitting blouse fastened by three brooches worn by Malay women
mooncakes	Round crusts of pastry filled with bean paste and melon or lotus seeds; eaten during the Mooncake or Lantern festival
sarung	Loose, ankle-length skirt neatly folded and tucked securely around the waist traditionally worn by Malay women and men
satay	Malay dish consisting of small, spicy pieces of beef, chicken, or mutton skewered on thin sticks, barbequed over a charcoal fire, and dipped in peanut sauce
sumatras	Sudden violent storms
Temasek	"Sea Town" or port; possibly original name of Singapore

INDEX

101